Aquatic Landscaping

From Ordinary Tank to Extraordinary Ecosystem and Modern
Aquascaping Design

COLIN MOTLEY

TABLE OF CONTENTS

Introduction

This will be a "how-to guide" addressed to the knowledge of aquarium landscaping. Our whole goal will be to let you know in detail everything you need to know about how to switch from an ordinary tank to an extraordinary Ecosystem and modern Aquascaping design.

This guide has been studied in detail to provide you with a complete overview of the subject and give you all the best advice and practices to be able to achieve this aquatic landscaping that you have long wanted to have.

Anyway, the guidebook will be divided into eleven main parts. Among these there will be:

1. How to get started: we will therefore start from the basics, to make you understand how it is best to proceed in this direction.

2. Lightening: the lighting part is vital when it comes to building your perfect aquatic landscaping. Here too, you will be guided step by step in choosing the right lighting.

3. Filtration, Circulation and Heating: this will also be a very explanatory part in which you will be shown how to carry out all these steps that will help you achieve your desired goal.

4. Feeding Aquarium Plants: this instead will be a specific part dedicated to the nutrition of what will make your aquarium truly spectacular, or how to feed your chosen plants correctly.

5. The importance of Carbon Dioxide: in this part of the guide, we will instead highlight the importance of this element for the perfect success of the aquarium landscaping.

6. How to Aquascape: here we get to the heart of the concept of Aquascaping, highlighting the traits and processes to make you real masters.

7. Hardscape: in this part we will go even deeper and reveal everything you need to know specifically about the hardscaping practice.

8. Choosing, preparing and maintaining your aquarium plants: these 3 fundamental steps will also be shown in detail, indicating valuable tips to make them better.

9. How to choose fish shrimps and snails: after you have chosen the flora of your dream aquarium, it is also right that you choose the fauna that will have to stay in it and, thanks to our advice you will be able to make an accurate and apt choice.

10. Different Fish species conviviality: in this part of the guide, we will explain to you how to create a jovial and functional atmosphere of coexistence among the fish you decide to insert in your aquarium.

11. Maintenance: in this final chapter, however, we will talk about more general maintenance, so that your aquatic landscaping can not only take the shape you want but it can also have longevity and remain beautiful and intact over time.

As you can see, each part of this practical guide will be very specific and will deal with every single issue and eventuality. At the end of this reading, we are sure that you will become a real Master of Aquatic Landscaping. You just have to start reading and find out everything you need to know to transform your aquarium into something truly electrifying and spectacular. You will be envied by all! Enjoy the reading...

Part 1: How to get started?

In this first part of the guide, we will provide you with the basic information required to learn more about the world of Aquascaping and how to get started in the right way.

Basic definitions

To start with the basics, let's start with some definitions:

Aquarium

The aquarium can be defined in general as a transparent container that can allow the breeding of fish, mollusks, crustaceans, and amphibians but also, concurrently, the cultivation of aquatic or marsh plants. It is usually shown in the shape of a parallelepiped but has dimensions that can vary from a few decimeters on each side to a few meters, but also different shapes. The size of the tank must be adapted to the type of flora and fauna with which you want to populate it. So, it's something highly subjective and personal. As we will see better below, the most used material for the walls of an aquarium is made up of glass plates, even if in recent decades tanks made of plastic materials such as Plexiglas have become widespread. In addition to the tank, the aquarium normally has filters, a heat producer with a thermostat, and a lighting system that is almost always equipped with a timer to automatically adjust the switching on and off of the lights. But how to achieve all this, will be discussed in the next chapters.

Aquascaping

Aquascaping encompasses everything related to the admirable natural processes that take place in an aquarium and, through creativity, develops real works of art.

Aquascaping therefore means knowing well the "natural rules" dictated by the aquarium hobby, adapting and organizing them in suggestive natural settings.

Inside there are various techniques, tools and styles.

When we do Aquascape we are artists or "aquascapes", and everyone develops their creativity differently, regardless of the techniques and tools we use.

As Takashi Amano, creator, and founder of Aquascaping teach us, the foundation for starting to develop a natural aquarium lies in observing nature and learning from it. Indeed, from the 90s onwards, in fact, Aquascaping has come a long way from distant Asia up to our aquariums. It has mutated more and more from a niche to a popular phenomenon. Today, through numerous international Aquascaping competitions, and companies in the sector that have created a series of specialized products,

Aquascaping is an expanding sector with an increasingly prosperous future. Some evolutions are already being seen now, such as the more detailed creation of mountain landscapes, woods and forests.

Aquascaping is, therefore, summing up, the art of creating or furnishing one's aquarium with suggestive settings, of great scenic impact in the eyes of the passionate aquarist; the combination of luxuriant plants, the arrangement of the rocks up to the choice of animals (in exceptional cases) are part of an aquarium philosophy that is increasingly gaining ground in Italy as has already happened and is still happening abroad. In this guide, we give you the concerted opportunity to recreate this spectacular art form right in your own home.

Why Aquascaping?

The aquarium is not only, as we have just said above, a glass container that houses fish and plants, with the sole task of beautifying our homes. We think that this still widespread general view needs to be corrected.

An aquarium is an art. It is a small natural world that develops within a closed ecosystem.

There is one thing you should know; the management of this closed ecosystem is not only about the welfare of the fish but will be above all the result of how we will control and take care of everything around plants and fish inside and at the base of their habitat. For this, Aquascaping comes into play which, with all its practices and nuances, allows you to make your aquarium a real work of art. Aquascaping, unfortunately still considered by many to be a passing fad, is a very concrete branch of fishkeeping that opens up new scenarios not only for the market but also for "creativity" in the passionate aquarist, now fed up with the usual tanks with fish freshwater or marine and, in constant search for new solutions, innovative in some respects. If you find yourself in what we have just told you, you can only continue reading to create your dream aquarium step by step.

Getting started: types of aquariums

But returning to the discussion of aquariums and how to start making your own, know that it is also important to evaluate the types in use. Among enthusiasts who are dedicated to aquarium keeping as hobbies, two large families have usually used: freshwater aquariums and saltwater aquariums, also called marine. Then there are separate, niche categories, such as brackish water aquariums and paludariums, the latter being similar in concept to reptile houses.

But, in more detail, different ecosystems are made by aquarists, listed below:

Freshwater aquarium

Aquariums where fish and plants of different families and species that belong to the habitats of freshwater biotopes are hosted.

Marine aquarium

A saltwater aquarium requires much more complex and expensive equipment, among these the most sought after are the reef aquariums in which the habitat of the tropical coral reef is reconstructed.

Artificial aquarium

Compared to any other aquarium, here you don't have living beings, but plastic elements that reproduce the features of marine beings, where to be able to move them, you use a pump that creates a current flow in the aquarium by moving the water or through the air.

Anyway, the correct position of the aquarium is closely linked to its size, but some general indications are always valid. As we will see in the next paragraphs, the ideal place to put the aquarium should have light and temperature conditions that are as uniform as possible.

Choice based on the Structure

Even when it comes to choosing, the structure is important, and looking at the top, aquariums are divided into:

Open

Where it is possible to admire the aquarium from above and to cultivate plants that exceed the surface of the water (e.g., Echinodorus) or live on the surface of the water (e.g., Lemna minor), but which require suspended ceiling lights for lighting. The intense evaporation requires frequent top-ups of water, demineralized so as not to dangerously change the chemical parameters.

Forced Aquarium

Open or closed aquarium with a cavity under the sand drained by a pump, can have an internal or external filter also connected to the sand filter. Recommended ventilation and the presence of a waterfall to renew the water on the surface, especially if the presence of plants is limited. If set up with slow, fast-growing plants and populated in moderation, it guarantees chemical stability even around 30°, a temperature which, however, is rarely reached in aquariums with common fish. Given high evaporation, very soft or osmotic water is preferable. It does not require frequent fertilization, and even exposed to direct sunlight it does not present excessive algae formation, except in the case of lack of balance, mostly caused by excess nutrients. If constantly monitored, active maintenance requires few interventions even after 6 months for filter cleaning (fortnightly evaporation top-up).

Closed

They are more separated from the home environment, essential for breeding jumping fish (e.g. fish accepts). The lighting is very simple: neon tubes (but short-lived and high consumption) or LEDs, sometimes included in the lid. Evaporation is limited.

To get started: where to place an aquarium at home

For beginning your journey of Aquascaping and creating a modern and spectacular aquarium, you must know, as well as possible shapes and structures, above all where to correctly place an aquarium at home. Because this choice, in addition to personal taste and the style of the furniture, also depends on other variables. Placing an aquarium in an apartment is a decision closely linked, first of all, to set up the furniture.

However, we must not forget that we are talking about a particular habitat in which living beings and plants must be contained, so its position must consider the needs of the animal and plant species hosted. Having said that all depends on your taste and the style of the furniture, other variables must be considered. Sometimes it happens to see aquariums that are perfectly integrated into the context of the furnishings, but do not leave the space necessary to carry out the most basic maintenance operations, such as opening the lid.

But if you think there are too many variables to evaluate, don't be discouraged. Ask a technician from a specialized shop for advice and you will more easily find the place to put the aquarium in your home.

The important thing is to choose the right place because from there you will no longer be able to move it, except at the cost of considerable inconvenience.

But in addition to talking about the places in the house, where you could insert the aquarium, let's also talk about those where you absolutely must not put an aquarium.

In the environment in which fish and other living organisms move, sounds and above all vibrations are of particular importance. For this reason, it is necessary to keep the aquarium away from sound sources such as:

✓ Television
✓ Freezers and refrigerators
✓ Stereo system

✓ Home theatre, etc.

It is therefore important to place it away from equipment that can produce vibrations.

The aquarium should not be placed in a smoky place such as the kitchen. Water is in fact a solvent and fumes and fats produced by cooking food can easily flow into it.

In moderate amounts, light from a window can be beneficial; excessive radiation from the sun can, on the other hand, cause an increase in water temperature.

For this reason, the tub should be kept away from the window and direct light sources. There is nothing more dangerous for the health of fish than the increase in water temperature, which causes a decrease in the oxygen present in it and excessive proliferation of algae.

For the same reasons, the water tanks with fish, even if they are equipped with thermostats for regulating the internal temperature, must be kept away from heat sources, such as stoves and radiators. Also avoid places where drafts may be present. For avoiding stressing the fish, avoid placing the aquarium in the most chaotic places in the house, such as the corridors which, as passageways, are busy. It will seem obvious, but I advise you not to place the aquarium near fine carpets. Sooner or later, it can always happen that a little water falls.

Likewise, be careful with furniture and floors that are particularly sensitive to liquids. In fact, consider that many aquariums are filled with sea water, so there is also saltiness.

In any case, the position of the aquarium must necessarily be next to a power socket, to allow the operation of all its utilities:

✓ Lights
✓ Pump
✓ Heater
✓ Aerator.

It would be advisable, even if more difficult, to also have a water point nearby, given that the operations of filling, cleaning and partial changes require the water supply.

The position of the aquarium must in any case be such as to leave enough space to carry out periodic cleaning and maintenance operations.

Always to start. How to choose the furniture for an aquarium?

Keeping on talking about the basis, is right to address you on the right furniture choice. Small or large, each aquarium must be placed on a suitable support, to be observed at the right height.

The piece of furniture on which to put the aquarium must be sturdy and resistant. Consider that a 50-liter aquarium can weigh, with all the internal set-up, around 60 kg, but some home aquariums can even weigh 150 kg.

Another important feature of the furniture must be its resistance to humidity. The wooden supports must be specially treated or covered with waterproofing materials, otherwise they could swell and deform over time due to the absorbed water, with the risk of collapsing.

Adequate resistance to saltiness is required for the marine aquarium, so if the support is made of metal, it must necessarily be stainless.

To avoid any mistake, choose specific supports for the aquarium and above all avoid placing it on a trolley with wheels to move around the house.

Regardless of the place where you decide to put your aquarium, remember to place the tank on a slab of at least 5 mm thick polystyrene or neoprene. This arrangement has several advantages:

- ✓ Thermally insulates the bottom of the aquarium.
- ✓ Helps to dampen small vibrations.
- ✓ Prevents small imperfections on the shelf where the glass is placed from causing it to crack under the weight of the tub.

How to start Aquascaping?

Aquascaping is not as many believe, neither difficult nor so expensive in terms of money and time. It is simply the next artistic step, after understanding the basics and mechanisms of managing an aquarium.

Difficulty, time and money depend exclusively on the qualitative result to be obtained. However, creating a low-cost and medium-easy-to-manage tank setup is accessible to everyone.

Our main advice is to start off on the right foot, following the right advice, thus avoiding loss of money and having to restart an aquarium from scratch.

Here are the main steps to start doing your business.

Tank

We think the choice of tank is not vital for the result, it all relies on the space available and our initial budget.

In any case, to move from an ordinary tub to a modern and spatial ecosystem, you must choose the right tub for the environment in which it is to be positioned, as well as personal taste. An aquarium is not an ornament because it contains living beings and therefore it is important to choose the right size in proportion to the quantity of fish and the species to be introduced. Furthermore, it is also important to know that each type of fish has different needs for space and setting, so the choice of the tank must never be underestimated.

To give an indicative measure, it can be said that different types of fish can be introduced into a 200-liter aquarium, but if it is the first aquarium that you set up, it is advisable to start with a smaller tank. For example, 100 liters are sufficient for Platy, Coridoras, Mollies and similar fish to live adequately and healthily. A great way to start learning about the amazing world of aquariums.

But if there is any advice we want to provide you, is to not begin either with tanks that are too big and difficult to keep and higher in cost, or with tanks that are too little (under 30 liters). These little tanks are dangerous because it's harder to keep a definitive balance in the water values (above all during the start-up phase). In general, however, it can be said that for the construction of Aquascaping tanks, open aquariums are used, with all glass sides and without any plastic parts. The ideal is a tub with a width that is at least half the length, and a height at least equal to the width. These dimensions make it possible to arrange the elements on different levels to create a sense of depth. On the contrary, the use of aquariums that are too tall or narrow is strongly recommended.

The Set Up

But choosing the size of the tank is not enough, you then need to know how to set it up and prepare it so that it is a suitable habitat for the fish.

Setting up an aquarium for freshwater fish must be done carefully and respecting the times necessary to create an adequate microclimate for the life of fish and plants. The first set-up must be performed by obtaining the material for the seabed, therefore peat, gravel and sand. Furthermore, lime-free water specially selected to be suitable for this use must be used. Tap water is no good.

Set-Up materials

Consider the materials divided into two sections.

1. Fund: the choice of substrate is fundamental for the growth of many rooting plants (e.g., CryptoCorine) and for the release of nutrients. We, therefore, recommend starting with fairly simple

sands and gravels (still providing balanced fertilization) to make the "start-up" of the tank easier. Furthermore, immediately obtained a better aesthetic result.

2. Rocks and woods: there are various types of rocks and woods, and their choice depends a lot on the aesthetic result that is designed. We only advise you to be careful of types of calcareous rocks that can change the chemical characteristics of your water and at the same time many roots can create contrary situations and turbidity. Attention: almost all the roots will need to purge for a period ranging from one week to one month and will create harmless whitish patinas (e.g., mucilage) and cloudiness. We recommend purging them before placing them in the aquarium.

Filters and pump

In addition to the bottom and the water, you must get the filter and the pump, essential accessories to keep the water clean and continuously oxygenate it. The filter must be changed regularly and the pump clean and always running. The more experienced often do not keep a backup so as not to leave the fish without oxygen and filtering in case of failure. Once the base has been created and the water has been introduced into the tank, one must wait at least 15 days for the harmful elements inside to be neutralized. After that, fish and plants are added.

The filter and the pump are two essential parts of the aquarium, whatever the type, size and position, these two mechanisms can never be missing. Their function is to keep the water clean and oxygenated, to create an ideal habitat for fish. Otherwise, the water would become dirty in which bacteria and harmful substances would form, making the fish sick and dying. Furthermore, by applying the filter and pump for the aquarium, there will be a perfect distribution of food and good gas exchange between the water and the environment. Not to be forgotten is the light which is usually already included on the lid of the aquarium and the power is calculated about the size of the tank. The temperature must also be monitored with the appropriate thermostat that heats the water adequately.

Accessories

The selection of accessories relies on the characteristics of the tub and the result you want to achieve. In addition to a good filtration system and a thermostat heater, it will be necessary to achieve the right balance between lighting - co2 - fertilization.

In this regard, our advice is not to flaunt savings on these three elements. They will be essential to obtain good results with plants and in general with a good balance in our tank.

Plants and fish

Well, this is the fundamental choice to make, but we want to refer you to the appropriate chapters to better understand how this choice should be taken.

Finally, to get started you need the right accessories

To finish this chapter, let's see what the main tools are and how they are used, starting right from the setup phase of the aquarium:

✓ The "sand flattener" is used in the early stages of setting up, in the creation of the hardscape, to level the substrate giving it the right slopes and to adapt it to the furnishings so that it fills the empty spaces and that the composition is more natural. But in reality, it is always useful because often both after water changes and after a light siphoning off the bottom there is a need to recompact the substrate and the decorative sand when present.

✓ Indispensables are the tweezers for planting, there are all sizes and different shapes to be used according to the aquatic plants that are going to be planted. The smallest and most pointed are foreground plants which have a very slender root system and must be planted stem by stem. Those with the larger, rounded tip are useful for planting plants with larger root systems such as CryptoCorine and Echinodorus, but also for stem plants as they have a wider and better grip on the tip and more can be inserted into the substrate one stem at a time.

✓ Some tweezers have an inclined tip to allow planting close to rocks and roots. For the pruning of the plants, it is important to use strong and sharp scissors of excellent quality so that the cut is clean and precise so that the cicatrization takes place as quickly as possible. This consideration is somewhat valid for all species and above all in the initial phase when a little more structural pruning is carried out, looking less at aesthetics and layout.

✓ Shears with wider blades are used above all for stem plants and for formation and containment pruning, for example when large Rotala bushes need to be shaped. Those with a short blade can instead be used in cases where greater strength is needed, for example to cut the roots of epiphytic plants or the leaves of anubias.

✓ The wave-shaped scissors are very handy: indispensable for pruning lawn plants in the foreground and for reaching otherwise inaccessible spaces, and very useful in small aquariums.

✓ The "spring scissors" are beautiful with their very comfortable spring cutting system that allows you to carry out quick and precise interventions. They are used for pruning mosses which need frequent interventions to thicken and maintain their shape.

In this chapter, we were able to understand how the aquarium hobby is capturing the attention of millions of people from all over the world. Modern life pushes us more and more to have pets at home, because it's fascinating to keep a corner of nature at home. Besides this, it is a hobby where every person finds something interesting to devote time to in a particular branch. And we've told you how to get started. In the next chapter, we will talk about a very important aspect of your business, namely the correct choice of lighting.

Part 2: Lightening

After talking about the basics of aquascaping and how to get started, let's talk more specifically about lighting. We will show you, very briefly, some tips for choosing the right lighting for your aquarium.

Lightening: some useful tip

As far as lighting is concerned, for example, in general, it would be good to position it to receive light indirectly, so that the fish can gradually get used to the transition from the dark of the night to the light of the day.

For example, you could choose a place in the dark in a lateral position concerning a window or French door. Proper lighting helps recreate the natural day-night cycle inside the aquarium. Plants need light to carry out photosynthesis, removing nutrients from the water. If this didn't happen, the algae would proliferate affecting the quality of the water, and the health of the fish and the other inhabitants of the aquarium. But is daylight enough to illuminate my aquarium? Natural daylight alone is not enough for your aquarium. You must ensure that you do not expose the aquarium to either direct or indirect sunlight as the temperature of the water may rise significantly causing the algae to spread.

Also remember that, to understand and choose the right lighting for your aquarium, there are rules to respect, and you need to know these fundamental elements which are generally reported in the specifications of the lamps that are on the market, as those we will see below. The choice of lighting for an aquarium is extremely important for the health of plants, fish and other aquatic life. This is why it is important when buying lamps for an aquarium to know all the aspects to take into consideration. LED lighting is the most energy-efficient option for an aquarium installation, but there are other aspects to consider such as the color of the light and the duration of the lighting. LEDs, as we will see specifically below, offer significantly lower energy consumption and, at the same time, a better quality of light. Furthermore, the LED tubes do not generate heat in the light emission. This helps extend their life by up to 3 times longer than neon tubes. The LEDs are also available in G13 (T8) and G5 (T5) sockets, making the transition to LEDs particularly easy. However, know that, to give you a quick calculation, the recommendation for the amount of light in the aquarium is around 30 lumens per liter of water. This allows most plants to thrive in the aquarium. Since some plants need even more light to grow, you can provide up to 50 lumens per liter. Even plants that need more light will be able to grow in peace.

The value of 30-50 lumens per liter is, however, a generalized estimate. How much light an aquarium actually needs depends entirely on the type of plant used.

Too bright light in the aquarium can lead to more algae growth, but too little light can hurt plant growth and health. In fact, if you increase the intensity of the light, the plants will carry out more photosynthesis and consequently, they will need more CO_2 and nutrients.

For those who are wondering at this point, what color temperature to choose for an aquarium?

In general, the following applies: The light color 'daylight' is best suited for illuminating aquariums. It is the light closest to sunlight and has the best combination of red and blue wavelengths. Both are necessary for balanced plant growth. In addition, the blue light penetrates deeper into the water and can therefore also illuminate the bottom of the aquarium. Aquatic plants also process a higher percentage of blue light for photosynthesis, as more of it reaches them. Red light is spectrally filtered by water and is therefore not very useful for aquarium lighting.

The color of light or color temperature is measured in Kelvin. The lower the Kelvin value, the greater the red component in the light. Since we need daylight white light for the aquarium, LED tubes with a color temperature of 6,500 K to 8,000 K are recommended.

For the colors in the aquarium to be reproduced naturally, the color rendering index (CRI) is a decisive factor when choosing LED lighting. Ideally, an E is recommended finally for those who want to know CRI between 80 and 89 or even better 90 and 99. This means that all colors are reproduced in all their liveliness and naturalness.

Finally, for those who want to know how long the aquarium light should stay on, a lighting duration of 8-10 hours is ideal. This ensures that the day-night cycle is respected. Plants need a minimum light period of 6 hours to be able, for example, to carry out sufficient photosynthesis. Make sure the lighting does not exceed 12 hours. In freshwater aquariums it is also possible to take a short break of up to 4 hours during which the light can remain off. It is advisable to avoid this break with marine aquariums.

What types of light to choose?

As we all know, light is essential for animal and vegetable life (chlorophyll photosynthesis) and the choices we find on the market concern the following lamps: HQI bulb projectors, NEON T5 T8 or PL tube linear fluorescent lamps (bent lamps), or on LED ceiling lights. Before listing the main differences between the three types and explaining what the photoperiod, lumens, color temperature, and color rendering index are, you need to know that thanks to light, all the chemical reactions that allow both the recycling of nutrients and the development of plants, as well as the correct development of invertebrates and fish, giving rise to the so-called "nitrogen cycle".

HQI Lamps: By now of an old generation, they have a not very high purchase cost, but unfortunately due to their poor energy efficiency they have a very high electricity consumption, moreover they heat the surface of the water a lot, which in winter can be an advantage. but in the summer a disadvantage. Unique value? the light emitted is very diffused, but it must be changed at least once a year.

✓ detailot2 NEON T5 T8 or PL tube lamps: They can be a valid alternative to HQI since they consume slightly less even if their energy efficiency is not optimal, they too raise the water temperature since they radiate heat, and must be combined to have certain spectra luminous, they have a very low purchase price, but unfortunately, they have to be replaced once every 6 months. The light emitted is very diffused.

✓ 1474534991Led ceiling lights: They represent a large initial investment (we can even exceed 2000 dollars) but they have excellent luminous efficiency, as electricity consumption will be really low and will not increase the water temperature. Furthermore, the Led ceiling lights can bring out the fluorescent colors of the fish more and are generally already combined for all possible spectrums and kelvin gradations, often they are equipped with control units that will reproduce sunrise, day, sunset and moon phases, and once purchased, if good quality, should never be changed. The only characteristic defect of the LED is the emanation of punctiform rather than diffused light, the efficiency and duration instead depend on the cooling, the more it will be cooled and the longer it will last over time.

✓ dfssdfdLUMEN: It is the unit of measurement that indicates the quantity of luminous energy that is emitted by the lamp in the unit of time. Many will have happened to notice that lamps of identical wattage but of different brands can produce light of different intensities perceived by our eyes, why? The reason simply lies in the luminous efficiency of the lamp which is given by the ratio between Lumen and Watt. A good ratio, so a good light efficiency is 60 – 80 Lumen/Watt. To have good lighting, especially for planted aquariums, a ratio of 0.5 Watt/Liter will therefore be sought, in aquariums with little planting, it may be lower, but it must never be less than 0.2 Watt/Liter.

✓ Color temperature, kelvin degrees: To understand what "Colour Temperature" is, let's take a cold iron bar as an example and heat it to very high temperatures; during this process it will go through a vast range of colors, all corresponding to a certain temperature expressed in Kelvin degrees, which will go from red to yellow, then white, green, light blue and blue and all intermediate shades. Taking into account that the color temperature of sunlight in nature is around 5500° Kelvin, if we need to stimulate the growth of plants we will opt for Phyto stimulant lamps which will have a color temperature of around 3000° Kelvin or shades of red pink , if, on the other hand, we need a lamp that brings out the colors of the fish and gives the sensation of strong sunlight, we will adopt a whiter and more intense color around 6500° Kelvin. It is often recommended to combine both types to complete a wider range and satisfy both needs, the important thing is that the color temperature range for a freshwater aquarium is 3000° – 6500° Kelvin.

- ✓ 3COLOR RENDERING INDEX – IRC – RA: This parameter, also indicated with the abbreviations IRC or RA, indicates the percentage of the light that illuminates an object that allows our eye to perceive the real color of the object in a precise way. object itself. For this to happen, the wavelength of the light we use must be compatible with the color of the object we want to illuminate. This is why it becomes essential to have more lamps that will allow us to cover a wider part of the light spectrum by recreating a light that is as close as possible to the natural light of a certain moment of the day (usually noon).

- ✓ Photoperiod: The term photoperiod means the lighting period and therefore the duration of lighting of the lamps in the aquarium; generally, it is about 8 – 10 hours a day and can be managed both manually and with the help of timers. In our experience, a longer photoperiod can create algae problems and it will be advisable to recreate the sunrise and sunset effect, both for an aesthetic factor and to avoid creating stress for the animals in the tank. Therefore, if you adopt HQI or Neon bulb lamps, we recommend turning on the lights progressively, not all at the same time, instead of LED ceiling lights, there are control units and remote controls that will allow you to choose the intensity, color and many other parameters, for this reason they are highly recommended.

This concludes our chapter on lighting. In the next we will address another important topic for Aquascaping or the choice of the right filtration, circulation and heating.

Part 3: Filtration, Circulation and Heating

In this section we will deal with talking about other fundamental choice features for your aquarium or filtration, circulation, and heating systems.

Filtration

The filter always remains the heart of the aquarium and it is necessary to understand it well so that it can work at its best. In simple terms: first, the coarse waste is blocked in the filter, then the harmful substances are broken down and "digested" by the bacterial flora that lives there.

This process takes place through these kids of filtration: biological, mechanical, and chemical. Not all filters, as we will see later, have all these filters.

A simple diagram will help us to understand better:

- ✓ Water entry
- ✓ Heater
- ✓ Mechanical filtering
- ✓ Mechanical/biological filtration
- ✓ Biological filtering
- ✓ Centrifugal pump

Let's see in detail each step related to the points indicated above.

Water entry

Its function is obvious: to allow water to enter the filter. Its slots mustn't be clogged with dead leaves or other debris that would impede the flow of water.

Heater

It is the "stove" of our fish; it must be calibrated based on the optimal temperature of the organisms we host (usually between 23 and 28°C). Beware of summer temperature changes and very cold winter days.

Perlon wool

It is usually sold in bags, very similar to cotton wool packs. Be careful not to confuse them: cotton wool is not good as filter wool because it clogs easily, blocking the flow of water.

Its function is to collect suspended particles (fish droppings, dead leaves, food leftovers, bottom dust, debris, and sediments...) so that they do not clog the other filtering materials.

Filtering

This is the beginning of the "true filter". Filtering is possible thanks to different materials that participate in water purification.

The first distinction to be made to identify the various types of filters are:

1. Mechanical filter
2. Biological filter

The mechanical filter

The mechanical action filter mainly takes care of simply removing dirt particles, such as plant residues, uneaten food, and excrement.

Generally, the water flow flows quickly and the collected parts are treated by sponges or Perlon which will be rinsed often.

This type of filter usually has one or a maximum of 2 types of filter materials: sponges and hair.

When different materials are present, they usually have a different ability to hold dirt.

Sponges can have more or less small pores and therefore be able to retain dirt of different sizes: the sponge with the smallest pores should be placed close to the pump, while the others closest to the water inlet. Perlon wool typically holds more coarsely and is usually the first filter material the water will pass through in the filter.

For what about maintenance of a mechanical filter, the filtering material tends to get dirty quickly and therefore needs to be cleaned often. To clean it you must not use tap water, but it is better to use aquarium water: just, when changing the water, collect the water in a basin and use it to rinse the sponges and the Perlon several times and then put it all back together.

Mechanical filtration is typical of small quarantine tanks or for the growth of fry, but it is not a complete filtration system as, both due to the speed of passage of the water and the lack of suitable supports, it does not allow settlement of nitrifying bacteria in it.

Biological filtration

The filters that are already set up in the aquariums that we find on sale, are normally biologically active. They can be internal or external filters and consist of various areas for the insertion of filtering materials which, crossed by the water, perform their function of purification from harmful substances. The main difference between mechanical filtration and biological filtration is the presence, inside the filter, of an area containing a substrate for the settlement of nitrifying bacteria. This substrate is generally the last one before the pump, in a dark area and is made up of razor clams, bio balls or other special supports.

The biological filter typically contains:

✓ Perlon
✓ Sponges
✓ Battery holder
✓ Pump

They are often sold with charcoal as well: it is not necessary. It should be used only in special cases, in case of pathologies and use of medicines and removed once its function is completed.

The water entering the filter must follow a path:

✓ It is cleaned of larger particles, such as food residues, leaves, etc. Through the Perlon
✓ It is cleaned of the finest particles by several layers of sponges with pores of different sizes
✓ It passes in the area of the razor clams (or similar) where the bacteria have settled
✓ Through the pump it returns to the aquarium

A deepening of the action of bacteria has been addressed in these articles that I invite you to read:

✓ Slow nitrogen cycle and biological filtration
✓ Guide to the freshwater aquarium
✓ The most common aquarium filters
✓ Filtering in the aquarium

In regard maintenance of a biological filter, since the first part of the materials performs a mechanical action inside the filter, these materials must be cleaned quite often, to prevent the filter from clogging and the water from no longer being able to circulate.

You don't have to use tap water, but when you change the water, use the water collected from the tub to rinse the sponges and then put them back in their place.

Rarely and, usually, after several years if the initial part of the filter is well structured, it is possible to notice some brown sludge in the area of the razor clams: it is very normal and does not preclude the functionality of the filter.

If you want, you can clean the filter container, again with aquarium water, taking care to never leave the razor clams in the air, but always immersed in the aquarium water and possibly in the dark. The razor clams or any other support for the bacteria should never be washed or rinsed: it would only mean throwing away most of the bacteria themselves and starting the maturation of the aquarium again, even if only partially.

Chemical filtration

As a further and last stage of filtering, before the pump, chemical filtering can be provided which allows the removal of chemical substances dissolved in water, such as for example ammonium, silicates, phosphates, coloring substances, etc.

This is normally obtained through the use of particular resins, each of which performs a precise function; there are anti-silicates, anti-nitrates, and anti-phosphates and they invent new ones every day.

Anti nitrate resin

Many aquarists shudder at the idea of using resins or similar materials because they are "unnatural". In fact, if the aquarium wants to be as faithful a representation as possible of an ecosystem, eliminating waste products using "chemical" substances is nonsense.

However, chemical filtration allows you to keep overcrowded tanks healthy, or to eliminate toxic substances or substances that have accumulated due to incorrect management from the water. Not to mention the removal of medicines when you are forced to use them.

The latter effect is normally obtained through activated carbon sponges which are also useful for removing any excess coloring substances or fertilizers.

Activated carbon sponge

If you use them, bear in mind that the adsorbing power runs out in a short time; therefore, if the problem is not solved, they must be replaced.

We propose a natural management of the aquarium; for this reason, we advise you to remove carbon and various resins from the filter and to use them only in case of actual need.

Centrifugal pump

This is the "muscle" of our filter. Thanks to its suction and consequent delivery of water, it allows all the recirculation in our aquarium. Many pumps allow the flow rate to be adjusted.

If you see a decrease in flow, disassemble the pump and clean it of any debris or accumulated algae.

How to choose a proper filter

When choosing the aquarium filter, it is always advisable to also consider other characteristics such as:

1. The filter volume: the space available for the filter materials
2. The flow rate: how much water is moved by the pump in one hour
3. Consumption: the watts used
4. The head: for external filters it indicates how low it can be positioned concerning the aquarium. In fact, if the filter were positioned lower than the prevalence, the pump would not be able to return the sucked water into the aquarium.
5. The dimensions: to understand how much space it will occupy inside the aquarium or if it fits in the cabinet in the case of external filters
6. Silence: it can become fundamental if, for example, we decide to keep the aquarium in the bedroom.

For points 1 to 5 you can easily refer to the card of the filter we want to buy.

Circulation

When we talk about circulation, we refer to pumps. A very important element for every aquarium, in fact, is the pump. Aquarium pumps perform a very important function: to promote the circulation and movement of water within the aquarium itself, helping to keep it healthy.

Mainly, aquarium pumps can be divided into two macro-categories: delivery pumps and movement pumps.

Delivery pumps

The delivery pumps perform the function of facilitating the recirculation of water from the aquarium sump. There are submersible and dry delivery pumps. Immersion ones are quick to assemble and generally cheaper. As it is obvious to see, they are installed directly inside the sump. Dry pumps, on the other hand, are installed outside the sump and generally connected via a watertight fitting. While, as anticipated, the immersion delivery pumps greatly facilitate the work (especially for the more experienced users), the dry pumps have pros and cons:

✓ PROS: being external to the aquarium, they do not influence the water temperature with their operation
✓ CONS: they tend to be more expensive, and the pond connection can cause water loss problems in the medium and long term

Movement pumps

Already from the name, it is easy to understand the crucial role of movement pumps: to simulate the movement of currents, to drag various impurities, food residues and excess organic materials.

The movement pumps allow the water to maintain a state of cleanliness and correct oxygenation. As with delivery pumps, movement pumps are also generally divided into two types: submersible pumps, located directly in the aquarium, and external pumps, usually installed on the outside of the aquarium itself.

Power and use of pumps: Which pump to use?

In principle, it would be important to ensure that the power of the pumps in your aquarium is approximately equal to at least twenty times the flow rate in cubic meters of the tank.

Consequently, a 100-liter aquarium will need a power of around 2000 liters/hour, a 200-liter one with a power of around 4000 liters/hour and so on.

As far as the circulation of water is concerned, however, be careful! Regarding movement pumps, it is important that the recirculation is not limited to a single sector but gradually involves all the water contained in the aquarium.

For this purpose, it is particularly useful to take advantage of timers, customizing their activation so that the movement of the water is as articulated and homogeneous as possible.

Heating

A fundamental and essential element for an aquarium is the heating system composed of a heater and a thermostat which controls its temperature and consequently it's functioning. On the market these two devices are often joined together in a single body called a heater.

The optimal temperature to maintain is between 24° and 28° depending on the habitat and the type of animals present in the aquarium.

The water heater for the aquarium or aqua terrarium is one of the fundamental components that must almost always be present in an aquarium to guarantee the ideal temperature conditions for the fish or reptiles hosted. Only goldfish and/or cold-water fish do not need this item.

In winter, in the absence of a heater, the water could become so cold as to easily lead to the death of the aquarium guests after a slow cold that presents itself with white dots on the scales (ichthyophyriasis).

How does the aquarium heater work?

The operating principle of the aquarium water heater is very simple: inside the transparent glass casing (quality heaters have this Pyrex casing which is much more resistant to heat and accidental blows) there is a resistance that turns on automatically through a simple electric circuit; in the upper part there is an adjustable thermostat similar to those used in the electric oven at home or in other household appliances; when the temperature drops below the set threshold, the thermostat opens the electric circuit and the resistance starts heating until the water reaches the desired temperature. Once the set value is reached, the resistance will switch off and then switch on again when the water temperature drops again due to heat dispersion in the aquarium or aqua terrarium. Usually, a good appliance has a sensitivity of 1°, that is: when the temperature drops by 1° the electric resistance will automatically switch on and then switch off again when the set value is reached. Using the plastic slider placed on top of the heater, set the required temperature.

To check that the heater is working correctly, it is recommended to use an aquarium thermometer which will be mounted, with the supplied suction cup, at a distance from the heater.

How to install a water heater in an aquarium?

Mounting the heater in the aquarium is very simple, in fact it is enough to apply it on the internal glass of the tank using the special suction cups supplied and then adjust the thermostat from its cursor, according to the desired temperature. If the aquarium is equipped with a biological filter, this will have a special compartment for the heater, indicated on the filter packaging.

The only precaution is to pay close attention to the water level in the aquarium which must be high enough to completely cover the lower part of the heater where the resistance is contained. However, the minimum and maximum water levels are indicated on the appliance.

If the heater is not immersed enough in the water, it will not heat well, as the thermostat will almost always switch off due to excessive heat which will only be dissipated into the air.

Do not pull out and even more do not touch the object when it is on as you may burn yourself.

A good heater that complies with current legislation must also have an automatic safety switch for self-shutdown after 120/180 seconds of operation out of the water.

How to choose the power of the heater?

The aquarium heater must be chosen according to the volume of water to be heated.

The right ratio is 1 watt for every 0.7 liters of water to be heated, i.e., a 100-liter net aquarium will need a 150 watt heater to ensure you always have the correct temperature in the water.

Now that we have stopped talking about these systems, the discussion will change in the next part of the guide and will focus on the nutrition of aquarium plants.

Part 4: Feeding Aquarium Plants

Let's see in this chapter what are the basic elements to know for the nutrition of aquarium plants and how to feed them.

Basic elements of aquarium plant nutrition

Let's see in a quick overview what are the highlights of growing plants in an aquarium.

1. The soil has relative importance for aquarium plants because most of them feed on the leaves, but in any case, it should not be neglected. The substrate material not only serves as a substrate to fix the roots of the plants but also as a deposit of a certain quantity of nutrients which subsequently dissolve in the water to be absorbed by the plants.
2. We have already spoken of light; without adequate lighting no plant can grow.
3. Nutrients are the third factor for plant growth. In addition to carbon dioxide for photosynthesis, plants need mineral salts dissolved in the water, many of which come from the decomposition of organic material that takes place in the filter; others must instead be administered by the aquarist through special fertilizers and/or nutritive soils.
4. Fertilizer for aquarium plants is essential for growing live aquatic plants and keeping them healthy. It is a useful product to administer the dose of nutrients they need to always be thriving. Different types of fertilizers are available on the market, liquid, in tablets or as a substrate, essential for having a beautiful aquarium to look at. As an aquarium evolves, the fertilizer dose should be adjusted regularly. The consumption of an aquarium will not be the same as soon as it is installed, when it has already been running for a few months and we have a large mass of plants or immediately after pruning. A 50% weekly water change is recommended to avoid the buildup of pollutants and the buildup of a specific nutrients.

How to understand if plants have nutritional deficiencies

If the growth of aquarium plants is stunted or even shows damage to their tissues, they generally suffer from a lack of nutrients or imbalances in the aquarium. It is not abnormal for these factors to appear in combination with increased algae growth.

Lack of Hydrogen

Nitrogen (N) can be absorbed by aquatic plants in various forms: ammonium, urea and nitrate. To determine the nitrogen content of water, we generally only have water tests that can indicate nitrogen in the form of nitrate (NO_3). The optimal concentrations are between 10 and 25 mg / l NO_3.

A typical symptom of a nitrogen deficiency is a general yellow discoloration of the plant, especially in the older leaves. New leaves getting smaller and smaller or stunted growth can also be an indication of a nitrogen deficiency. Some plant species take on a distinctly reddish hue. An increased presence of green thread algae, shrub algae or black beard is quite common when the aquarium is deficient in nitrogen. It is possible to increase the nitrogen supply with liquid fertilizers.

Lack of phosphorus

The concentration of this element in water is normally measured by taking the concentration of phosphate (PO_4). This is done with a commercially available water test. The symptoms of lacking phosphorus (P) can be noticed simply in fast-growing stem plants. He very slows the growth and the tips of the shoots that decrease in size are the most common bioindicators.

Some aquatic plants may turn darker or even purple. Often a phosphate deficiency can cause an increase in green dot algae. In a planted aquarium, phosphate concentrations of approximately 0.1 to 1 mg/L PO_4 are recommended. This substance does not need to be measurable and permanently kept in the water. Phosphate is quite reactive and can interact with other nutrients such as iron. Also, plants can store good phosphate. Excess phosphate in the aquarium can cause the appearance of stringy green algae.

Lack of potassium

Common for lack of potassium (K) are leaves with holes or dying leaf tissue (necrosis). At first, a potassium deficiency shows up as small black dots only, but then they turn into visible perforations, which are partially outlined in yellow or black, like a nitrogen deficiency, these bioindicators can show in Anubias, Hygrophylas and Ferns Furthermore, the leaves may turn yellow and show reduced growth. The excesses of potassium in aquarium plants can block the absorption of other plant nutrients, in addition, the new leaves grow twisted and stunted. Optimal potassium concentrations are 5 to 10 mg/L in water.

Lack of magnesium

Magnesium (Mg) has an important role in photosynthesis, and for this reason it is an important fragment of the green pigment (chlorophyll) of the plant. A lack of this element is often seen because of a pale or yellow discoloration of older leaves. On the contrary, leaf veins generally stay green.

Lack of micronutrients

Micronutrients are elements that plants need only in small quantities (mostly only as trace elements) for their proper growth. The most important of them is iron, but also other metals such as copper, boron, or manganese.

Lack of iron

When a lack of iron (Fe), plants will produce less chlorophyll in their new shoots. An iron lack can be simply identified in the shoot tips of fast-growing stem plants. The leaves are no longer green, and the shoots of the young plants acquire a color ranging from yellow to white and transparent. (chlorosis).

In the case of a severe iron deficiency, the stunted growth and dying black leaf tissue (necrosis). Deficiency symptoms can easily be eliminated by joining a little more iron fertilizer.

The ideal concentrations of iron for planted aquariums are given from 0.05 to 0.1 mg / l Fe, verifiable with the iron test.

Lack of light

Lack of light is rare in a balanced system. But it could be one of the sources of slow plant growth. A more focused look at nutrients from points 1 to 3 should have a much higher priority. The lighting requirements of the plants must correspond to the technical conditions of the aquarium. It can be a mild deficiency symptom. For example, extremely slow growth. Many plant species prefer a lot of light, such as most stem plants, but also some ground cover plants tend to sprout in low light conditions and the plant develops very long internodes. The distances between the two stem nodes are too long as the plant tries to achieve the right perspective.

Considering symptoms of deficiency in aquatic plants it is necessary to bear in mind that some optical factors can influence. You may see deficiency symptoms in your plants even if there is no reason. The color of the light source affects how you perceive the colors of your aquatic plants, such as green leaves. Light sources with a daylight spectrum of around 6500 Kelvin are neutral. Some pure white LEDs make bright greens very pale and whitish. This could be misinterpreted as chlorosis. Conversely, LED lamps with a higher RGB content enhance red tones, which look much less spectacular in a more neutral light. Another essential factor is referred to the angle of incidence at which a plant is looked into underwater. Seen from above across the surface of the water, even light green hues tend to look much lighter than the plant itself through the front glass.

How to feed aquarium plants?

The Law of the Minimum describes how plant growth is limited by limited resources. Plants need many different nutrients, so-called essential nutrients, to grow healthily. If only one of these nutrients is missing, plant growth will be inhibited, even if all other essential nutrients are available and in abundance.

This also applies to all other resources, such as light and CO_2 in quantities appropriate to the respective plant species. The scarcest resource always limits the growth of plants and hence, it is called the limiting factor.

We have named the four main factors for the good growth of aquarium plants in the previous points: Light, carbon (in the form of CO_2), macro and micronutrients.

If aquatic plants show signs of deficiencies, even in combination with intensive algae growth, the reason is usually an imbalance in the nutrient supply. Therefore, giving them lighter CO_2 will not result in better plant growth if another specific nutrient is deficient such as nitrogen or iron for example.

As a countermeasure, nutritional gaps (as those we mentioned above) need to be identified and filled. To do this, two things are important: firstly, the water parameters must be checked with the corresponding water tests and secondly, one must try to interpret the symptoms of visible deficiencies in the plants.

However, as we have already said, fertilizers prove to be fundamental when it comes to planting nutrition. It is an indispensable product for growing and keeping aquarium plants healthy which, to always be luxuriant, must receive the right amount of nutrients. In fact, just like fish, they too need to be scrupulously and carefully cared for. Everyone knows that fertilizers in the aquarium are important for plants, but very few can juggle the many products available, which have the most diverse characteristics and indications.

Used indiscriminately, fertilizers produce more harm than good in our tanks. A great expert explains why and how to avoid mistakes.

In fact, different types of fertilizers are available on the market: liquids, in taps, or as a substrate, let's find out together which are the best to use to ensure the well-being of aquatic plants.

As far as fertilization is concerned, we recommend not starting for one or two weeks after starting. Then you can start fertilizing according to the needs of your plants.

But you should be careful when you employ allophane lands (e.g., Akadama). In this case, you will encounter longer maturation times and changes in the structure of your water due to the absorption of salts by the bottom. Once the fund is saturated, the situation will begin to stabilize.

In this case we recommend a minimum maturation period of one and a half months and planting when the situation is stable. Many plants would not tolerate such low water hardness values.

After the discourse on plant nutrition, we are going to describe the importance of carbon dioxide in the next part.

Part 5: The importance of Carbon Dioxide

In this specific part of the guide, we will show the importance of carbon dioxide when it comes to aquariums.

What is carbon dioxide?

We briefly describe what carbon dioxide is and what it is used for.

Carbon dioxide is a molecule having CO_2 as its molecular formula. Although carbon dioxide is mainly found in gaseous form, it can also come in solid and liquid forms. It can only be solid when it is below -78 degrees C. Liquid carbon dioxide mainly exists when carbon dioxide is dissolved in water. Carbon dioxide is soluble in water only when pressure is maintained. As a result of pressure losses it tends to escape into the air, leaving a mass of air bubbles in the water.

CO_2 serves as an inert end product, which accumulates in the atmosphere and is in a continuous exchange relationship with the biosphere and oceans. Carbon dioxide reacts with water to become carbonic acid or hydrogen carbonate, which causes the alteration of the pH value, i.e. the degree of acidity of the water. Humans use carbon dioxide in many different ways. Carbon dioxide released by baking powder or yeast causes the batter to rise.

Some fire extinguishers use carbon dioxide because it is denser than air. Carbon dioxide can coat a fire, due to its heaviness. It prevents oxygen from feeding the fire and consequently the burning material is deprived of the oxygen it needs to continue burning. Carbon dioxide is one of the most abundant gases in the atmosphere. It plays an important role in the life processes of animals and plants, such as photosynthesis and respiration.

The importance of carbon dioxide in your aquarium

Carbon dioxide is, together with light and nutrients, one of the three fundamental elements for the care of plants in the aquarium. Carbon dioxide is a gas that we often find in aquariums, both fresh and marine, but let's try together to understand why and its importance. The solubility of this gas in water is in fact very low, as it tends to disperse from the environment in gaseous form, and this is why we add it through the micronization of pure CO_2 bubbles with specific diffusers, i.e. the so-called micronized of CO_2.

The lack of carbon dioxide makes the abundance of others useless; if in fact this is in low concentrations not all the iron added with the fertilizations will be absorbed by the plants, and the excess will remain available to the algae. As we have seen, carbon dioxide is important for plants (it is the source of carbon for all plants), but stopping at this concept alone is very simplistic. In reality, CO_2 plays a fundamental role in the chemistry of the aquarium and in particular affects the pH (acidity) and the KH (hardness).

In nature, carbon dioxide is never lacking (it derives from fish respiration, from infiltrations from the subsoil, etc.), in the aquarium, however, it is always insufficient due to the demands of the plants and the movement of water on the surface (which expels it). Aquatic plants in this situation tend to take carbon from the bicarbonates in solution through a process called "biogenic decalcification", thus lowering the carbonate hardness (KH). It is evident that this process has various negative consequences: the first is that, by extracting the carbon from the calcium bicarbonates, there will be a precipitation of calcium which forms a patina of limestone on the leaves. All this damages the metabolism of plants by preventing the process of chlorophyll photosynthesis. Another and perhaps more serious consequence is, given the buffering power of the KH on the pH, the possibility of having significant changes in the pH value. Since there is no longer any substance that controls the pH variation, it is possible to find a pH of 5 in the morning and 8 in the evening with imaginable consequences for the aquarium guests.

Administer CO2

After all this, the need to administer carbon dioxide directly appears evident, especially in the case of aquariums rich in plants. There are different types of CO_2 diffusion systems on the market today: those with cylinders, those that rely on fermentation, those based on electrolysis, etc. All guarantee an excellent emission, but how much should be administered? The optimal content of carbon dioxide in an aquarium ranges from 30 to 60 mg/lt (depending on the number of plants), to measure it just rely on a long-term test that will allow you to monitor the value at any time of the day.

Why add CO2?

In summary, carbon dioxide must be administered for two important reasons:

✓ Provide carbon to plants to start the process of chlorophyll photosynthesis
✓ Ensure a stable pH on slightly acidic values.

The addition of the CO_2 system is mostly done in heavily planted aquariums or that have the presence of fast-growing plants, as it favors chlorophyll photosynthesis, which takes place by aquatic plants. The quantity of CO_2 to be introduced into an aquarium, defined using a small formula, $CO_2 = 3*kh*10^{(7-ph)}$, from which derives a table that states, according to your Kh and Ph, how many Ppm of co3 to go into the tank, in the case of aqueous solutions, approximating the density of water to 1L/Kg, we have that 1ppm = 1mg/l.

But why do we take KH and pH into consideration for the administration of CO_2? We have said that the concentration of CO_2 in water tends to be very low, therefore aquatic plants in their evolution have also learned to use bicarbonates, which therefore present in water can function as a source of carbon. That's why the a close link between pH, KH and CO_2. In addition, CO_2 also has a function of a chemical nature, namely that of keeping pH and KH stable below 7.

The classic systems for placing in aquariums are:

✓ 500gr disposable CO_2 cylinder, with pressure gauge.
✓ Refillable cylinders generally 4/5kg always with pressure gauge but with the attachment for refillable cylinders
✓ Do-it-yourself kits, through the use of yeasts, citric acid and anything else using "arranged" instrumentation, work but often need maintenance and are not always constant in the emission.
✓ CO_2 kit by electrolysis, is a simple method but it becomes almost impossible to calibrate the amount of CO_2 emitted.

Finally, we would like to remind you that an aquarium full of healthy plants is an ideal habitat for all types of fish.

Having said this, our fifth part ends too. In the next one, the discussion will be further interesting because we will deal with Aquascape realization.

Part 6: How to Aquascape

Now let's see in detail all the practical steps to be able to Aquascape practice. We know, so far that building Aquascaping in an aquarium is a satisfactory experience as it calls for a combination of elements of design and biology. This combination is aimed to give birth to an amazing and healthy aquatic ecosystem.

How to start correctly

Starting an aquarium correctly is the basis for obtaining excellent results in our small underwater world. But it is also the basis for proper Aquascaping. Once you have begun an aqua setup, it's essential to plan by choosing the right kind of aquarium, equipment, and substrate.

Many do not consider the fact that, from filling the tank to putting the fish in, there are many biochemical processes in between. The aquarium will then undergo a maturation process, which is essential for creating the conditions necessary to host your future fish and thus establish a natural balance in the ecosystem. It is therefore not possible to add fish before this period!

The engine of many of these processes is different strains of bacteria. I will not go into overly articulated and complex speeches concerning more specifically scientific branches, but I would like to briefly present what is happening.

Nitrogen cycle

One of the processes that underlie the maturation of our aquariums concerns the so-called "nitrogen cycle". The aquarium, is in charge of the aquatic balance in managing the waste produced by living beings.

You have almost certainly heard of Ammonium (NH_4), Nitrites (NO_2) and Nitrates (NO_3) in the aquarist field. They are chemicals that form the basis of the nitrogen cycle that takes place in the aquarium. The process has the task of transforming the most polluting toxic substances (ammonium, nitrites) into less aggressive substances (nitrates) and then partially eliminating them (releasing nitrogen into the atmosphere).

The engine of this cycle is represented by three types of bacteria:

1. The first genus of bacteria, called Nitrosomonas, will take care of transforming carbon dioxide into organic carbon, using the ionic energy which transforms the ammonium present into nitrites. NH_4 to NO_2

2. A second genus of bacteria, called Nitrobacter, will oxidize the Nitrites present in Nitrates. NO2 to NO3

3. A third group of denitrifying bacteria (Pseudomonas, Clostridium) will be able to metabolize organic carbon thanks to nitrates and thus release gaseous nitrogen. The percentage of nitrates present in the water will therefore be reduced.

As already mentioned, I will not go further into too complex discussions since the number of cycles and processes that take place in an aquarium would be much larger.

The steps to follow to start an Aquascaping practice

Here are the main steps for your Aquascaping.

Water treatment

The water to be used for our aquarium can come from our tap, our osmosis system or both sources.

If you use tap water, you will first have to treat it with a bio-conditioner which will remove heavy and toxic substances such as chlorine and heavy metals.

If you use osmosis water, you will necessarily have to rebuild it according to your needs through specific salt supplements. Otherwise, you can go and cut it into halves/cuts with tap water if the latter is "hard" enough (high enough pH and total hardness). Obviously, it is always recommended to treat it with a bio-conditioner.

Filling

Once your water is ready, you can start filling your aquarium.

During this phase you can decide to start the tank empty or add plants, in the second case you can plant them by first moistening the bottom and the materials or filling the aquarium by about 5 cm with water.

If you have created a good layout with your materials and you have already inserted the bottom, be careful not to lift it or make the setup collapse with the jet of water, so I suggest you use a lid, a bag or some paper towels so as not to hit materials directly. If you insert roots that have not yet been drained and are mature, they will tend to float, therefore they will have to be fixed to the bottom. Once you have finished filling, activate your heater, filtration and, if you have one, your CO2 system.

Bacteria insertion

At one point your aquarium has been filled and started: it will be necessary now to insert bacterial strains. There are products of various kinds containing bacteria that will populate our bottom and our filter and will take care of all the processes related to the nitrogen cycle.

They will be essential at an early stage and can be replenished during future water changes.

In this regard, in my shop, I offer highly selected products that contain colonies of LIVE bacteria already active and ready to populate your aquariums à Bacterial activators.

Maturation

After completing the previous steps, you just have to wait and let the ecosystem activate, I strongly recommend checking the chemical values through special tests to check the hardness and characteristics of your water. You can also check the values of Nitrites, Nitrates to verify that everything is going well (see the nitrogen cycle above).

Water changes

We recommend doing small water changes (5/10%) weekly starting from the second week based on your water characteristics. There could be cloudiness of the water, the appearance of mucilage on the wood and signs of activation of the bacterial flora.

These are normal signs during the maturation of the aquarium and over time the situation will stabilize, don't worry.

For aesthetic factors and/or the accumulation of fertilizing substances, I recommend small water changes.

Choice of flora and fauna

For this we refer you to the next chapters.

Fertilization

It is recommended, as we said in the previous chapter, not to start for one or two weeks after starting. Then you can start fertilizing according to the needs of your plants.

How to do real Aquascaping?

The term tank setup is a neologism that means "aquatic landscape". Aquascaping is a technique with which natural landscapes are created - as like life as possible - inside a freshwater aquarium. The tank setup is the most "natural" form of creating an aquatic landscape. In fact, a biotope is not created, that is the representation of an aquatic environment with plants, fish, wood and materials of a specific geographical place.

Aquascaping means creating real aquatic landscapes, furnishing your aquarium with suggestive settings and great scenic impact for the eyes.

At one point your tank is set up and planted: now the time to choose a tank setup style has arrived. Some of the more popular aquarium styles embrace the jungle style, the Dutch aquarium style, the Iwagumi style, the hardscape and the natural aquarium style. Every kind of style just mentioned has its aesthetic appeal and requires different types of fixtures and fittings. Let's analyze some of them specifically.

The Iwagumi

It is a style of tank setup. It was invented by Takashi Amano, the creator of the first natural aquariums.

It is completely referred to the principle of Japanese stone gardens, natural rock formations or landscapes are recreated in an Iwagumi aquarium. Takashi Amano has managed to apply these principles to an aquarium, creating a dynamic and particularly natural composition, through the positioning of the various stones inside the tank.

Iwagumi style tends to recreate natural rock formations with a minimalist style reminiscent of Japanese gardens. The Iwagumi style has a puristic approach and is characterized by a minimalist design. Based on this criterion, it is suggested to use only a particular type of stone as a decorative element. Aquatic plants are also used in this type of layout; however, the focus is mainly on the stones. The roots are not used.

This type of set-up is substantially made up of stones and must respect some fundamental principles:

✓ The rocks must all be of the same type, color and design, to homogenize and make the layout natural, but of different sizes (to learn more about the types of aquarium rock, look at the article dedicated to stones).

✓ The main rock, (the largest), must be positioned at 2/3 of the length of the tank, according to the golden rule. The remaining rocks will be positioned to climb trying to give maximum depth and naturalness to the panorama.

✓ The rocks must be odd, to balance and give harmony to the layout.

✓ When positioning the rocks, it will be necessary to look at the veins and orient them all in the same direction because even if they are of different sizes they will be linked together and will accentuate the direction of the water flow.

✓ The substrate material must be distributed among the rocks trying to give depth to the layout and having a thickness ranging from 2 -3 cm at the front to more than 10 - 20 cm towards the bottom.

In the Iwagumi installations, even if it is a subjective thing and depends on one's tastes, Takashi Amano always uses a few species of plants, often mixing them together. Eleocharis vivipara or Blyxa echinosperma, for the rear area instead Riccia fluitans, Glossostigma elatinoides, Echinodorus tenellus and Eleocharis parvula for the foreground, around the stones.

Aquascape Ryuboku

Ryuboku is another type of Aquascaping. Translatable into English with the expression "Driftwood", that is, "wood adrift", indicates aquariums set up with wood.

Takashi Amano has 3 types of compositions:

✓ Central, in which the woods are positioned perfectly in the center of the tank, forming a triangle with the vertex oriented upwards.

✓ Side, with the wood arranged in one of the two sides oriented towards the center to give dynamism.

✓ V-shaped, in which the wood is arranged along both sides, leaving an empty space in the center, to increase the sense of depth.

Hardscape

We will talk about this Aquascaping style in the next chapter.

Dutch Aquascape

The Dutch aquarium is a style of tank setup that has its origins in an association of aquarists, the NBAT - the Dutch Society for Aquarists, founded in Holland in 1930, and which has dictated the precise guidelines. Today, the Dutch style is very much practiced by aquascapes from all over the world. As for the characteristics of the Dutch tank setup, in general, Dutch aquariums are compared to underwater gardens. The main attention, in fact, is placed on the growth and arrangement of aquatic plants. In fact, the Dutch tank setup does not provide for the use of wood, rocks, or other materials for the hardscape.

The intricate placement and grouping of plants serve to create a depth perspective within the aquarium. To approach the style of the Dutch aquarium it is necessary - if not essential - to have an in-depth knowledge of aquatic plants since they represent - as mentioned above - the main materials used in Dutch Aquascaping. In addition to knowing and knowing how to choose the right plants, it is therefore equally important to know how to plant them, group them and combine them with each other, so as to create a pleasant and balanced final composition.

Generally, most Dutch aquariums are characterized by many plants that give life to a rich color contrast. The most used plants for a Dutch aquarium are:

✓ Hygrofilia corymbosa and Limnophila aquatica: large stem plants that grow quickly

✓ Lobelia cardinalis and Saurus cernuus: low growing plants

✓ Cryptocoryne (lucens, walkeri, wendtii, lutea and becketii): used in the first two rows of the aquarium and give a good contrast.

✓ Java Moss: Often placed between groups of plants to create contrast.

For focal areas, plants such as Alternanthera reineckii, Ammania gracilis 'golden' (Nesaea) and Rotala of all varieties can be used. Large plants such as Aponogetons or Lotus tiger are also fine.

Dutch Aquascape also follows the rule of thirds: dutch aquascapers, passionate about the Dutch style must know and apply the "rule of thirds", a guideline concerning the composition of visual images. Referring to these guidelines, an image should be thought of as if it were split into 9 equal parts. Of these 9 parts two are equally spaced horizontal lines and 2 equidistant vertical lines. This creates interest and energy in the composition, rather than simply focusing on the main subject.

Finally, as is true for tank setup in general, also for the Dutch aquarium, you can use both a closed aquarium and an open tank, preferably in extra clear glass.

Aquascape rocks

In the aquarium hobby, rocks, intended as a decorative element, have always been used. With the progress of Aquascaping, the request has become richer, especially as regards shapes and qualities. To set up an aquarium it is essential to know the characteristics of the various stones to know - or at least be able to imagine - the aesthetic effect that we are going to achieve. It is also essential to know the chemical characteristics of the various rocks within the biosystem.

What kind of rock do you put in the aquarium?

Here are the main rock classes:

✓ Sedimentary

✓ Igneous

✓ Basaltic

✓ Metamorphic

Let's see below which are the most famous and common stones for setting up.

Dragon stone

With color ranging from brown to dark yellow, with red or green reflections, it is a very light stone because it is full of holes and inlets. Takashi Amano often used the Dragon stone, together with the Seiryu stones and the Mountain stones. Dragon stone is perfect for epiphytic plants that attach themselves to it very quickly. Furthermore, since it does not release carbonates, it does not alter the water values.

Seiryu stone and Mountain stone

Rocks of calcareous origin are among the most used in Takashi Amano's installations. The color ranges from dark gray to light gray, with white veins. Full of inlets and holes, they recall rocky landscapes. Both of these stones are ideal for epiphytic plants and Iwagumi-style arrangements. Unfortunately, being of calcareous origin, they release carbonates, thus altering the water values. For this reason, before proceeding with the creation of the layout, it is advisable to place the rocks in a solution of 30% hydrochloric acid Hcl with water and leave it to act for 3-4 days. In this way, the external part of the rock will release fewer carbonates once in the tank.

Lava or volcanic rock

Natural aggregations of lava origin, are very light and very porous. Obviously, this benefits the total weight of the glass of the tank. These are rocks of excellent quality also because they do not alter the water values.

Slate or Blackboard

Quite light, this rock originates from thin layers of silt. With a very elegant shape, it is mainly composed of slabs, which allows us to offer large smooth surfaces. The color is very dark, usually black or dark green, with some white veins. Slate does not release carbonates and therefore does not alter the water values.

Quartz

A mineral that occurs in various forms. Generally, for aquascape setups it is preferred in the form of small pebbles or gravel, to compose the substrate. It does not release carbonates and therefore does not change the water values. Aesthetically, it has a somewhat "fake" effect.

Rainbow rock

With a very lively color, usually white and orange or white and red, these are stones of sedimentary origin, and which derive from Mexico. Sometimes they are artificially punctured to favor the attachment of epiphytic plants. They are ideal rocks for installations as they do not release carbonates.

Pagoda rock

With an excellent aesthetic result, this type of rock is made up of several layers of gray and brown. Almost reminiscent of wood. Pagoda rock also does not release carbonates into the water.

Sodalite rock

Also known as "silicate stone", it is very colorful (usually blue, red and yellow). It does not alter the water values because it does not release carbonates. Due to its showy coloring, for some it can create a slightly too excessive effect. But, of course, it all depends on personal tastes and the final result you want to achieve.

Aquascape: rock treatment

Now that we have seen the main types of rock used for tank setup, let's explain the treatment to which to subject them before immersing them in the tank.

First of all, it is necessary to know with certainty the degree of alkalinity of the rocks and the possible release of elements as they could influence and compromise the water values in the tank. If in doubt, carry out the carbonate test independently. Just put a drop of descaled or muriatic acid and see what happens. Then observe any "sizzling" reaction. The stronger this is, the more alkaline the stone will be, and therefore it will release carbonates into the water which will raise the pH, GH (water hardness) and KH (carbonate hardness) values.

After that, proceed with a thorough washing under running water, perhaps with the help of a brush, to eliminate debris or any animals inside them.

Finally, the rocks must be boiled in water for at least half an hour, to eliminate any pathogenic elements, such as bacteria or tiny insects.

A little FAQ

To conclude this chapter on how to do Aquascaping here is a small FAQ where we will clarify some further doubts.

How to create unevenness in the aquarium?

Creating unevenness is quite simple. Just use pieces of Plexiglas to arrange vertically and hide on the bottom. Alternatively, it is also possible to insert rocks – partially or completely – into the bottom. Surely, between the two alternatives, the option of rocks is better because they are part of the layout and integrate very well with it.

How to give depth to an aquarium?

To obtain the sense of depth you need to use many groups of plants in the central part and then continue outwards using very thin plants.

What bottom to put in the aquarium?

At the bottom of the aquarium, two components must be placed: sand or gravel, as a support to fix the plants and, below it, the nutrient substrate that provides the right amount of nutrients useful for the good maintenance of the plants themselves.
How to calculate how much bottom is needed in an aquarium?

The bottom, in addition to providing nourishment and support to the plants, is also decorative. To create a layout, it is necessary to create an inclined plane towards the front of the aquarium, thus placing a greater quantity of materials on the back (about 10-12 cm) and less on the front (about 6 cm or even less).
To calculate the bottom, it all depends on the height of the gravel you want to put.

How long to boil aquarium stones?

If the purpose is to sterilize them, the rocks must be boiled for at least 30 minutes. Shorter times do not guarantee sterilization.

What to put under the rocks in the aquarium?

In the case of very large and heavy rocks, something should be placed under the sand, such as a plexiglass plate, polystyrene or inert clay. On the one hand, the total thickness of the bottom of the aquarium is increased and it also prevents the rocks from being in direct contact with the glass.

How do you clean aquarium rocks?

In the case of soft or very porous rocks, just rinse them in running water by shaking them often. Otherwise, leave them to soak for a few days so that any agglomerations of clay or earth will melt, making them easier to remove.

In the seventh part we will look at the practice of hardscape.

Part 7: Hardscape

Now let's see in more detail what the hardscape consists of.

What is hardscape?

The hardscape is literally the "structure" of an aquarium, therefore its backbone and the starting point for its construction. In fact, it has the function of defining the layout of the tank right from the start, which will characterize it throughout its life.

Therefore, being the most important part of our home aquarium design, it will in fact be definitive and durable over time. The hardscape is therefore one of the main elements of the art of tank setup or also called water embellishment.

In particular, the hardscape is the main decoration and design work of the aquarium. It is referred to as the non-living part, made up of rocks, woods and other decorative similar elements. Hardscape elements can also provide shelter for any fish you wish to place in the tank and add visual interest to your tank, making it nothing short of spectacular.

At this point it is easy to deduce that by Hardscape we mean an aquarium layout made of gravel, rocks, tree roots and other decorations: therefore, by hardscape, we mean a construct without plants.

How to do it?

The hardscape, in practice, consists in choosing a suitable substrate for your tank setup. Depending on the style you choose, you can opt for soil or sand substrates or a combination of both. In addition to providing nutrients, soil can also help maintain the pH levels in your aquarium.

Once you've chosen your substrate, it's time to add some hardscape elements like rocks and wood. As we said, hardscape elements act as a shelter for fish and other aquatic life and give a unique style to your aquarium.

Having said that, let us tell you that there is no precise way to make a hardscape: therefore, know that its creation depends solely and exclusively on your imagination. But, following some general lines, as we all know by now the perspective and the differences in height between the back and front of the tank are very important, so you will create, for Aquascaping, supports for any stones or wood, using thicknesses such as polystyrene, Perlon wool, porous gravel or lateritic pieces. The important thing to note when placing these materials is not to make them match the edges of the tub, which would cause unsightly effects from the front and side points of view. Also remember that the thickness of the front must not exceed 2 / 3 cm in order not to be unsightly.

After having chosen the most visible point of the tank, you will begin to position our "hardscape", which in this context represents the bone and structural part, all of which will remain unchanged. You will build with wood or stones, according to the golden rule, a sort of V or triangle which will have as apex, in height, the part furthest from the point of view. You will also install the water jet so that the flow creates a movement of the vegetation, from the highest rear point to the lowest front point. If you decide to use heavy stones and rocks as a decorative material, also know that the Styrofoam should be placed on the bottom of the aquarium before the substrate. this is to ensure that the glass of your tub is well protected.

What to do after the hardscape: create your dream water tank

After structuring the hardscape, fill the areas with aggregates in this sequence:

- ✓ A layer of porous gravel will serve to allow the flow of oxygenated water in the normally anaerobic areas and allow the correct nourishment to the roots of the plants and the proliferation of nitrifying bacteria such as Nitrosomonas and Nitrobacter.
- ✓ Spread powdered fertilizer or fertile soil to allow the plants to draw nourishment not only from the water but also from the soil.
- ✓ The last layer is generally composed of allophone earth or fertilized earth for the areas to be planted or sand or inert cosmetic gravel, always respecting the unevenness. Remember to use the fertilized part for planting and the cosmetic part for the lower points of view, also be careful not to create anaerobic areas and therefore dangerous for bacteria, with too high layers of inert gravel. Minimize the cosmetic front layer, max 1/2cm.

At this point you are ready to add all the necessary details, i.e., aggregates of various sizes and small gravel, to be inserted into the rocks or to be placed on the paths. They are usually composed of the same material used for hardscapes such as crushed stones or small woods and are used to make everything more natural and like the reality of nature. Pay close attention to the shape and colors of the latter and make sure they are appropriate as it is the details that make the difference. After the part of "Hardscape" begins the planting or the insertion of plants in the soil or the sand. There are so-called "first and second floor" plants depending on their growth in height or width, furthermore you will need to know the specific characteristics and light requirements to choose places more or less exposed to light and more or less deep in the column of water. After having put a little water in the aquarium to make your work easier, you will plant in the substrate, with the appropriate tools, the second-floor ones or those with higher stems, in the rear part trying to accommodate the flow of the current. After that you will move on to the foreground plants in the front, i.e. the lower and often ground cover plants. As we will see better in the next part of the guide, there are other plants, the so-called "epiphytes" that do not need to be placed in the substrate and can be attached using wires that will be removed later or embedded in furnishings such as wood and stones, over time they will tend to cling to objects with their roots. Last tip, remember to contrast the colors well to give greater depth to your composition and above all always keep in mind the proportions of the leaves about the aquarium, so if you want to create a landscape "seen from afar" use leafy plants and small stem, if instead you want to create a glimpse "seen up close" such as a riverbed or a biotope then use plants with large stems and leaves.

Useful tips to create an ideal hardscape

Now that we have reached this point in our guide, let's see some final tips useful for making an excellent hardscape. If you want an aquarium only with non-living decorative elements, we want to show you all the elements we know about this vital underwater element, and how to take care of all the things present in your aquarium.

So, let's see what are the best advice: these tips will serve to keep well in your aquarium and get a good hardscape-based decoration.

Taking care of the health of fishes

You certainly know, if you've kept some aquarium before, that fish are sensitive animals to any commute or issue in the water parameters.

The water therefore must respect some features adjusted and adapted to what the fish needs. These features must also respect the parameters the fishes get in their natural habitat.

With all that we mean is that if we are thinking of inserting wood, rocks, or a new substrate in the water of an aquarium that is already a fish village, we must make sure to clean it well with neutral water before they enter. So, if we decide to clean rock with soap, we create contaminated aquarium water with a toxic element that will bring our fish to be sick at the moment.

The right proportion of the different elements

The second tip is not to exaggerate with the disproportion and not get bear away by the enthusiasm of the purchase and insert too many elements.

This is because aquariums shouldn't have all their space invaded; the reason why is that fish require to move and have balance and proportionality: the same free space, but also that is occupied by other elements such as plants or rocks or wood. The same goes for plants: if a plant gets too big it begins to occupy a space that takes away from the fish. So be logical, buy decorative elements that are proportionate to the overall size of your aquarium. That fish has both open spaces and decorative elements that give them hidden places. And if you wish to add new elements, new plants, or new fish, then the best thing is that you buy a larger aquarium with more water inside.

Variety and Simplicity

If you intend to have many fishes, you will try to balance the number of plants and the number of rocks. If you intend to have a few fish, you can logically increase the number of other parts, but always without overwhelming them and taking away the minimum living space.

The variety of elements is important in an aquarium inhabited by fish, as well as simplicity: this will allow you not to go crazy and incorporate things at random.

But when it comes to dealing with variety, we also mean to try new items if the first chosen ones don't work. So don't be mulish in a settled aesthetic that you might have thought of before you started: varied if one type of plant doesn't work for you, or if a rock or wood is wrong in size.

After the hardscape discourse, in the next part of the guide we will deal with one of the fundamental elements of our dream aquarium, or plants.

Part 8: Choosing, preparing and maintaining your aquarium plants

In this part of the guide, we will focus on the choice, care and maintenance of the plants in our aquarium.

Choose the right plants

The first thing you need to know is that when choosing plants for your aquarium, it's important to choose species that suit the size and environment of the tank. If you have already selected the materials and have already learned the basics of how to start an aquarium, then it is time to put in the plants. These will be the basis of your aquarium ecosystem, moreover, since it is Aquascaping, it is important to understand which ones to select and where to place them inside the tank, as their growth must be controlled to avoid distorting your starting layout.

To obtain excellent results and create your perfect tank setup, we recommend equipping yourself with a CO_2 system, good lighting and a fertilization plan. You can go and modify everything according to the needs of your plants. This does not mean that if you are going to insert some plants in the aquarium you will necessarily have to meet all the requirements described above in fact, there are slow-growing and easy-to-manage plants that, in the right aquatic balance, will be able to grow reasonably well. In this regard, I recommend fewer demanding plants with medium slow growth of the genera Anubias, Microsorum, Bolbitis, Cryptocoryne, and Echinodorus. I also recommend the Eleocharis so mini which can be a good option to create a carpet on the front, and many kinds of mosses that will add an extra touch to your tank setup, covering roots and setting up or creating carpets.

These are good alternatives if you don't have enough time and budget to get started.

However, I remind you not to flaunt the savings of good lighting, a good CO_2 system and a fertilization plan, because they are the basis for obtaining luxuriant growth and the benefits will be very evident, moreover many species of plants will need more attention in this regard. For this, refer to the previous chapters of the guide.

But let's see specifically what type of plants you could choose for your desired aquarium.

Epiphytes

The aquatic plants preferred by those who practice Aquascaping are the Epiphytes because they offer various advantages. Let's see them below.

They are exceptional from an aesthetic point of view because they recreate natural environments in an irreplaceable way while at the same time giving a magnificent naturalness to the layout:

✓ They are easy to grow
✓ They adapt to different light and CO2 conditions
✓ Once tied to roots and woods, they can be moved to change the layout
✓ They can be placed in any area of the aquarium (foreground, background, bottom near the substrate, top tied to the woods...)

What about, the characteristics of epiphytic plants, they have particular roots, made up of thin capillaries. For this reason, to be grown in the aquarium, they must be anchored to supports, such as rocks or wood. Just like aquatic mosses.

You also should know that epiphytic plants are the most used species for tank setup So let's find out now which species are most loved by aquarists and cultivated in the aquarium.

1. Anubias. Anubias are used very often both for Aquascaping layouts but also in tropical aquariums. They are among the easiest species to grow because they adapt to various water conditions. In particular, they manage to grow at a temperature between 20° and 35°, a PH between 6 and 8 and a KH between 3 and 15. Furthermore, the anubias can be placed in various areas of the aquarium, both

in the shade and under bright light. The Bonsai variety, with its tiny leaves, is one of the aquascapes favorite plants. Often, in fact, they use it at the bases of the woods and in shaded areas where other species would find it difficult to grow.

2. Bolbitis. The Bolbitis, originally from West Africa, are often used by tank setups who want to recreate aquatic landscapes inspired by forests and riverbanks. These are ferns with leaves that can reach 30 cm. Bolbitis adapts to living and growing in waters with temperatures between 15 and 28 degrees, PH between 6 and 7.5, and KH between 3 and 10. With good water movement, it grows faster. Under intense light, the leaves tend to thin and take on a lighter color.

3. Microsorum. Plants native to Southeast Asia propagate easily in water. The various species of Microsorum are easy to grow and adapt to a variety of conditions. They grow well in water with a temperature between 15 and 28 degrees, PH between 6 and 7.5 and KH between 3 and 10. The cultivars with thinner leaves are much loved by aquascapes. They are very useful when you want to represent thick vegetation or when it is necessary to have thick bushes in the middle of the branches of the woods. The older leaves often tend to turn black; for this reason, they must be pruned regularly.

Epiphytic plants are therefore one of the most suitable kinds for Aquascaping. In nature they grow on top of other plants or are anchored to rocks and woods. We will therefore have to arrange for their positioning in the tank on set-up materials and to cover crevices between wood and rocks. Avoid burying rhizomes and roots.

Mosses

There are several species of mosses (Taxiphyllum Barbieri, Vesicularia dubyana, etc.) that will be instrumental in providing a totally natural look to your aquarium. These can be anchored or glued in any position of the tank to cover ravines, roots and rocks. There is also the Cladophora aegagropila, similar to moss but belonging to the algae family, which can also be used in the foreground. We also recommend

Riccardia sp. "chamedryfolia", a more complex moss to manage than those mentioned above, widely used to form spectacular carpets. A good choice for beginners is hardy aquatic mosses and ferns such as Java moss, Christmas moss or flame moss.

The mosses will tend to expand covering the surfaces on which they rest and have a medium-slow growth. They prefer areas in dim light or any case not in direct light.

Japanese-style tank setup plants

For the Japanese style, in addition to Java moss, plants such as Eleocharis acicularis, Eleocharis parvula, Echinodorus tenellus, Glossostigma elatinoides, Hemianthus callitrichoides, Riccia fluitans and Staurogyne are mainly used. Also recommended are plants with linear and ribbon-like leaves, such as Eleocharis vivipara or Vallisneria nana.

It might be useful to know that Takashi Amano uses only a few types of plants for most of his installations. It is recommended to choose 5/6 different types of plants which, above all, require the same values.

Setting and preparing your plants

Once you've chosen your plants, it's time to prepare the substrate and soil. A dark substrate with iron-rich soil provides a good foundation for aquatic plants. First, simply spread the substrate evenly over the bottom of the aquarium. Then carefully place each plant in the desired location with tweezers. Creating an Aquascape using soil and substrate is an essential part of setting up the perfect right aquarium. A type of volcanic ash substrate, it is the best choice for Aquascaping in an aquarium. It furnishes a bigger surface area for beneficial bacteria to grow, helps lower and stabilize pH, and provides essential plant nutrients.

When you are installing an aquarium, as we have already said, the first step is to fill it with water. After filling the tank, add soil and substrate in layers. Start by applying a thin layer of gravel, followed by a layer of soil. This will aim on avoiding the water become cloudy. Once the soil and substrate are in place, it's time to start planting your aquatic plants.

For best results, choose aquatic plants suitable for small aquariums, such as anubias and java moss. Start by planting smaller species towards the back of the tank and larger ones towards the front. Make sure you leave enough space between the plants to allow them to grow properly. Be careful when planting your aquatic plants as root damage can cause stunted growth or death to your plants.

When Aquascaping your tank, take the time to put your plants in an aesthetically beautiful way. Try to create a balanced composition with different heights and textures to emphasize the beauty of your tank setup.

Now let's see a possible and recommended setting, where they will be positioned in the aquarium.

1. FIRST FLOOR: At the front of your tub you can place low plants, which can create carpets. Strong lighting will be necessary (except in some cases) for the plants to develop correctly. Here are some of my recommendations on some plants that you can use:

   ✓ Eleocharis parvula (or Acicularis mini) - Micranthemum sp. Montecarlo
   ✓ Hemianthus callitrichoides "Cuba" - Glossostigma elatinoides
   ✓ Lilaeopsis brasiliensis - Utricolaria graminifolia

2. SECOND FLOOR: In the central part we will have all the epiphytes, mosses and plants of the Cryptocoryne genus. The latter will be very important for the absorption of the substances from the bottom as they are very rooting; moreover, many varieties can also be used in the foreground and background. We also recommend other plants such as:

   ✓ Pogostemon Helferi - Eleocharis Acicularis
   ✓ Alternanthera reinekii "mini" - Sagittaria subulata
   ✓ Helantium tenellum green - Rotala macranda "red mini"
   ✓ Hydrocotyle verticillata

3. THIRD FLOOR (BACKGROUND): In the back it is very common, as well as recommended, to use stem plants. They are fast-growing plants that will be able to create bushes and groups in the rear area, I also particularly recommend placing this type of plant in the tank especially if you have just started the aquarium; they will in fact be able to buffer any excesses of nitrites and nitrates during the "startup" phase. Here are some examples of plants you can use:

   ✓ Rotala sp green - Limnophila hippuridoides
   ✓ Limnophila sessiliflora (and/or heterophylla) - Ludwigia repens
   ✓ Rotala rotundifolia - Ludwigia arcuata
   ✓ Rotala Vietnam
   ✓ Rotala points

Other plants to use in the foreground or background can be rooting plants of the genus Echinodorus and Vallisneria.

There are many other species belonging to these three groups described above, we also want to clarify that this list is just an example to order ideas if you don't know which plants to buy to set up your aquarium. We therefore invite you to change your choices based on your tank, your goal and your management skills.

Maintaining your plants

The care of the aquatic plant is quite simple, for them to develop and thrive, some important rules must be followed. Aquatic plants are plants adapted to live with submerged foliage. Some of them still manage to survive and vegetate with the crown emerging. This form of adaptation is especially typical of riparian plants which are subject to seasonal 'immersions'. There are also many other subdivisions among aquatic plants.

First of all, a distinction must be made between real aquatic plants, algae (for example marimo) and aquatic mosses (for example Taxiphyllum). Algae and aquatic mosses have less resistance to terrestrial life. While some plants can resist a dry as long as humid environment.

Aquatic plants can extract the carbon dioxide necessary to carry out photosynthesis directly from the water. Nutrient elements are also 'fished' from the water or searched for through the roots within the growth substrate. During the day, their leaves will be covered in bubbles of oxygen, a sign that they are photosynthesizing.

Every aquatic plant needs a certain amount of light. There are outdoor plants that need direct sunlight. Other aquatic plants, on the other hand, can resist much lower light conditions.

When planting in an Aquascaping, in fact, it's also important to consider the lighting requirements. Most aquatic plants require adequate light for optimal growth, so equip your aquarium with an appropriate LED light source that matches your favorite species. The light should be aimed at the center of the tank so that all plants get sufficient light.

The species that come from tropical areas cannot survive outside our home walls and for this reason they must be kept inside during the cold season.

There are large plants and small plants. If you intend or are setting up an underwater landscape, remember to place the highest ones in the background and the lowest ones in the foreground.

Some aquatic plants can live both 'well planted' in the substrate and floating, i.e. floating. If you have floating plants, you don't need a growing medium.

Finally, make sure you are maintaining the correct water parameters such as pH, temperature and general hardness levels in your aquarium with regular water changes and testing. With proper care and maintenance, your aquarium will stay healthy and look great for years to come!

10 basic rules for the care of the aquatic plant

Here, summarizing what we have just said and adding more, what are the 10 essential rules for the care of your plants for Aquascaping.

1. Light is the plant's only source of energy, place your plant in a bright place but without direct sunlight.
2. The water temperature must be room temperature, neither too cold nor too hot, try to keep it below 20-22 °C.
3. Tap water is fine for most aquatic plants. Never use distilled water.
4. In summer, avoid placing plants in the hottest spots of the house, especially in the case of small aquariums.
5. From spring to summer your plants can be kept outside, in a position without direct sunlight. Beware of mosquitoes, they might appreciate the jars with the cap open!
6. The water should be changed every 15-30 days depending on the size of the container. We advise you to change at least half of the water. The small containers can be placed directly in the sink under the faucet. Take care not to open the water too hard so as not to undermine the plants. Any particles in suspension will then settle on the bottom.
7. When changing the water, clean the dead leaves, the algae along the inner walls of the jar and the limescale halos. To clean the walls, we advise you to use a paper towel, in the case of persistent halos, use alcohol.
8. If the water is cloudy, change the water and clean the container.
9. You can grow multiple plants together but pay attention to the size of the container. You can keep your marimos safely together with your aquatic plants.
10. The smell of an aquarium is important and will instantly give you the perception of some problem.

The eighth part of the guide is also finished. In the next one we will see what the fauna will be, and therefore the fish, shrimp and snails suitable for your aquarium.

Part 9: How to choose fish shrimps and snails

Let's see what other living species your aquarium will be populated with and how to choose them correctly.

After how would you be able to insert them?

There is no fixed and general vesting period. This is because each aquarium is different from the others and, on a biological level, can have slightly different characteristics.

It is usually recommended to wait on average for a month so that the tank can have the time necessary to balance its biological cycles and therefore allow the bacteria to settle the filtering materials and the bottom.

However, this period varies a lot based on how you start an aquarium, you will have reduced times if you follow the steps described in the lessons step by step.

Furthermore, I advise you again to focus on inserting live bacteria, as the times for bacterial settlement will significantly decrease.

To give you an indicative period, I advise you not to insert the fish for TWO weeks, or one month if you have the patience to get things done right.

This period will also depend on the number of fish you are going to insert.

How many fishes can you insert?

We strongly advise you not to enter all the fish you have selected at once, but to divide their entry into several groups. In this way you will avoid overloading your "biological filter" and will give it time to adapt to the presence of fish in the aquarium.

There is also no maximum number of fish to enter, this will depend on many factors such as the size of the tank, the different species and their compatibility.

We also recommend not overloading the aquarium as you will have short periods of time for water changes and you will therefore risk overloading with waste, compromising your biological balance, and you would also risk worsening any situations of incompatibility between the inhabitants.

How to choose shrimps and snails

Let's see how to choose and arrange the prawns in your aquarium.

Setting up a shrimp tank offers great fun and possibilities for many different individual setups. Below you will find all the tips for setting up your aquarium for shrimps or other crustaceans and how to make it an environment that respects the vital needs of its guests.

The choice of location

For aquarium guests to feel comfortable in your home, you will need to take into account some fundamental factors.

You need stable and flat support, insensitive to vibrations and placed near a socket to connect the technical equipment to. Do not place the aquarium in a position directly hit by the sun because the sun's rays could stimulate an undesirable development of algae and increase the water temperature in an uncontrolled way. A good location could be the corner of a room where there is no continuous passage which could scare the animals. In addition, a not too bright area will make your aquarium stand out more.

Background material

Once you have found the right location for your aquarium you can start furnishing it. For the bottom you will need aquarium gravel with a grain size of 1-3 mm. This gravel allows the roots of aquatic plants to become established but contains no nutrients. Before introducing the material into the tank, it must be rinsed thoroughly with water only. There are specific substrates on the market that favor the rooting of your plants and ensure the long-term presence of nourishment.

The temperature

The different species of shrimps, as well as the fish, have adapted over millions of years to the characteristics of their natural biotopes and therefore, to raise them in health, they must be raised in similar conditions. Only a few species, such as the "Red Fire", "bumblebee" or "Red crystal" Caridine, come from temperate or subtropical climatic regions, where the water temperature is between 15 and 25°C. There are numerous heaters on the market: powerful and safe, they ensure your aquarium a minimum water temperature, for the well-being of your guests.

Furniture

For the furnishing of an aquarium for small shrimps, in addition to gravel as background material and a few plants, one or more roots or a few twigs of dry wood, as well as dry leaves of beech or oak, can be recommended.

Not only do these items give the aquarium a decorative look but they also offer shrimp plenty of shelter and hiding opportunities. This material is rapidly colonized by countless microorganisms, such as Ciliates and Vorticella, microscopic worms and bacteria. These microorganisms are the natural food of small shrimps. By collecting this feed with the help of the fimbriated claws, the shrimps also ingest small fragments of the woody material which slowly decomposes: a healthy nourishment rich in fibers.

Snails

Making a beautiful aquarium does not mean only being able to reproduce a natural habitat with wood and rocks, as we have seen, but also adding all those details that make a tank even more beautiful: not only do fish populate the bottom of lakes and rivers, but many other living organisms are also added, for example snails.

Many aquariums set up without plants are perhaps just beautiful, completed with plants they are beautiful; they could become irresistible if, in addition to the fish, one could be seen spinning among the leaves beautiful snail intent on looking for food.

It must be remembered that these organisms are practically always present: from warm lakes to those of high mountains and their presence is almost always related to that of aquatic plants.

In reality, snails show an impressive degree of adaptation; fossils are found in millennia-old snails, they have evolved up to the present day by colonizing the warm waters, the cold ones and also the deepest waters. Let's try to search in gardens, lakes, or any if we can think of the probability of finding a snail or the sign of its passage is very high. Some snails live peacefully on the bottom of the lakes, others live in the interstices of the rock, others as external or internal parasites such as marine invertebrates, there are some snails move quietly on the seabed, and others are predators.

Variety of snails

Let's see a brief overview of the species of snails that can be introduced into an aquarium:

✓ Ampullaria australis, Ampullaria calculator, Ampullaria cuprina, and Ampullaria paludosa are perhaps some of the biggest snails that can be kept in a tank: it reaches 6 cm without problems diameter of the shell, which is orange in color, it is very easy to keep in the tank however it can also feed on the leaves of aquatic plants, especially with the shoots. He loves to eat salad that can be introduced into the tank tied to a stone to prevent the leaves from following the current of the water. In this species the sexes are separate, and the male is recognized because the lid he uses for closing inside the shell is convex in males and concave in females. This waste is the best indicator of water quality: when it goes to the surface and extracts some kind of proboscis to breathe the outside air means that the water is polluted or too rich in substances organic.

✓ Apple snail Planorbis cornesus, Segmentina victoriae and Marisa patella reproduce hermaphrodite snail very quickly; they can be recognized by its shell and has colors ranging from gray to dark red. The planabis corneus are shellless and absolutely unable to withstand a pH greater than 7.

✓ Planorbis cornesus, Melanoides turbeculata: a snail known for its cone-shaped shell no longer than 2.5 cm, is considered one of the best aquarium snails for its nocturnal activity of mixing of the bottom of the tank which in this way is oxygenated and facilitates the formation of denitrating bacteria in the bottom of the tank and thus helps the growth of plants they have stronger roots. It is a typical species of tropical freshwater aquariums; in fact, it hardly survives at temperatures below 18°C; it is native to South Asia and East Africa. If present in an aquarium multiply easily and you will find them everywhere even in the filter, if tend to move even during the day is an indication of pollution.

✓ Melanoides turbeculata Helisoma nigricans snail of Brazilian origin with a shell having a maximum size of 2 cm and colors ranging from red to dirty white, it is considered an excellent detrivore and rarely feeds on eaves of plants, it is hermaphroditic, and the eggs can be seen hanging under the leaves. Attention because with water below 20°C it risks death.

Ended this part, we will deal with different fish species conviviality.

Part 10: Different Fish species conviviality

Let's see how to solve possible problems with the different fish species conviviality.

Tips for managing conviviality

avoid, as the first main advice, mixing too many species! For example, if you buy schooling fish such as characins, concentrate on creating a minimum number of 8/10 specimens, avoiding including 2 of one species, 3 of another, and so on...

You will have to focus a lot on choosing species and their compatibility. Remember that the fish you are going to insert will be forced to live together in a closed ecosystem, so you will have to avoid inserting incompatible species as they will surely end up colliding or in any case stressing each other.

There are thousands of known species in aquariums so I can't give you a complete list, what I advise you is to select species that are already used to living in the same environment in nature.

Also evaluate the area they will occupy in the aquarium, for example some Corydoras will occupy the lower part of the aquarium, rummaging the bottom in search of food.

Families of fish such as characins will predominantly occupy the central part of your tank, so you can create schools in the upper middle area. Instead, fish such as Carnegiella will mainly occupy the surface area of the aquarium.

I therefore advise you to go and cover all three areas in the aquarium to create a balance between the species.

Snail problems

Often, however, if you talk to aquarists, the presence of snails in tanks is not well seen partly because they can eat the leaves of our plants partly because they believe, and sometimes they can be true, that they are carriers of parasites for the other tank guests. For this second problem, a simple solution suffices: when one collects in nature the specimens of snails wait for them to lay their eggs in a special tank prepared by us and then reinsert the mother snail into nature and keep all the other snails that were born from it eggs in this way the snails should not be carriers of disease; this method it only works if the snail's reproduction is asexual, in fact, snails generally are hermaphrodite.

Let's say that the parasites that snails carry before becoming dangerous for fish need to go through a series of intermediate hosts; in the way described above we interrupt the growing chain of parasites by eliminating some intermediate steps.

However, it is inadvisable to collect specimens in nature because they could carry parasites or of infections for humans so it is best to turn to producers who select their snails over years and always reproduce them in tanks in such a way that there can be no parasites dangerous.

Another negative aspect is that they also feed on eggs so if you intend to reproduce the fish in tanks it is essential to move them to a different aquarium.

After this brief discussion on conviviality, we will see, in the final chapter, how to do general maintenance of the aquarium.

Part 11: Maintenance

We have already talked about how to properly maintain plants in the aquarium. In this last chapter, however, we will briefly talk about how to do general maintenance of the aquarium, to ensure not only that you have perfect water, but also that you maintain the results in the long term.

Parameters of water in an aquarium

Checking the water parameters is important for proper maintenance in an aquarium. pH, GH, KH and TDS are the main parameters that need to be controlled. pH measures the acidity of water, GH is a measure of total water hardness, KH is a measure of carbonate hardness, and TDS is a measure of total dissolved solids. All of these parameters should be tested regularly to ensure they remain within acceptable levels for aquatic life.

Regular water changes are also important in an aquarium. Due to the smaller amount of water, partial water changes of 20-50 % should be performed at least once a week. This helps keep water levels in check and ensures there is enough oxygen for fish and other aquatic life.

In addition to monitoring the water values, the selection of suitable aquatic plants for an aquarium is also important. Aquascaping with live plants helps deliver oxygen to fish and creates an aesthetically pleasing waterscape. Long and short tanks are preferable because they are easier to tank because of their greater depth (width) front to back compared to height.

It is also important to use appropriate soil or substrate and lighting options for a successful aquarium setup. The soil or substrate contributes to the nutrition of aquatic life and allows for root growth in potted plants. Proper lighting will encourage plant growth and keep the tank vibrant and healthy.

Finally, regular maintenance and care are vital to maintaining a healthy aquarium. This includes cleaning the filter media regularly, replacing the filter media as needed, and regularly removing debris from the tank. It's also important to keep an eye out for algae growth, which can occur if the aquarium has too much light or if there are too many nutrients in the water. By following these tips, you can create a beautiful Aquascape with healthy water parameters that will provide you with hours of enjoyment!

Maintenance and care of your aquarium

For aquarists looking to maintain an aquarium, regular maintenance is the key to long-term success. To keep your aquarium healthy, you should perform a water change at least once a week. This helps keep the water chemistry balanced and reduces the chance of harmful bacteria developing in the tank. It's also important to make sure that the equipment is cleaned regularly and that any plants or dead fish are removed from the tank.

At the point to change the water, it is vital to employ dechlorinated water to avoid possible chemical problems. When changing the water, it is also important not to disturb the substrate too much to preserve the tank setup.

As far as lighting is concerned, it is best to use LED lights as they generate less heat than traditional incandescent bulbs and are more energy efficient. It is important not to place the aquarium in direct sunlight as this can cause algae problems and make it difficult for some aquatic plants to survive.

It is also important to check that all equipment such as filters, pumps and heaters are working properly. This can be useful in preventing potential issues in the tank before they happen.

Finally, it is important to regularly monitor nitrates and phosphates in the tank. High levels of these can cause algal blooms and stunt plant growth, so it's best to keep these levels as low as possible. Regular testing will help you spot potential issues before they turn serious.

Our complete guide on Aquascaping concludes with the maintenance of the aquarium.

Conclusions

At the beginning of this guide, we said to you that our main goal would be to let you know in detail everything you need to know about how to switch from an ordinary tank to an extraordinary Ecosystem and modern Aquascaping design.

For doing this, we have provided you with a complete overview of the subject and all the best advice and practices to be able to achieve this aquatic landscaping that you have long wanted to have.

For this we started from the fundamental bases to make you understand, in detail, how to arrange stones, rocks and plants inside your aquarium. When dealing with a real tank setup and therefore seeking a perfect balance in terms of layout, we recommend, in the end, inserting species, rocks and plants that do not distract the eye too much from the whole.

This is because there is a whole ecosystem to understand and discover and I think it is much more satisfying to focus on the view of an entire tank setup (including the fish that inhabit it) than to focus attention only on the fish, or the plants or the rocks. It must be a whole work of art.

The important thing we want you to know is that Aquascaping, despite our advice, is something that also follows our taste. Precisely because it is an art, it's up to you now to begin to understand how to set up the aquarium of your dreams. You have the basics, the information as well, and many, many tips to make your wish come true: all you have to do is get started!

Made in United States
Orlando, FL
13 July 2023

35103517R00039